Bigfoot

Written by
Jill Atkins

Illustrated by
Beatriz Castro

Published in 2026 by
Norwood House Press
2544 Clinton Street
Buffalo, NY 14224

Printed in the United States of America

Library of Congress Cataloging-in-Publication Data:
Names: Atkins, Jill (Children's author). | Rickard, Stephen, 1957-, author. | Castro, Beatriz, illustrator.
Title: Bigfoot / written by Jill Atkins, illustrated by Beatriz Castro. Toxic little critters / written by Stephen Rickard. Stunts are my thing / written by Stephen Rickard.
Description: Buffalo, NY : Norwood House Press, 2026. | Series: Phonics all-stars: phase 5a
Identifiers: ISBN 9781978578838 (pbk.) | ISBN 9781978578845 (library bound) | ISBN 9781978578852 (ebook)
Subjects: LCSH: Reading–Phonetic method–Juvenile fiction. | English language–Phonetics–Juvenile fiction. | Sasquatch–Juvenile fiction. | Dangerous animals–Juvenile fiction. | Stunt performers–Juvenile fiction.
Classification: LCC LB1573.3 A796 2026 | DDC 372.465–dc23

CPSIA compliance information: Batch #CW26NHP: For further information contact Norwood House Press at 1-800-237-9932.

"Look at this!" called Andrew, as he ran to the news stand.

Coral joined him. They stood reading the print.

"Some people reckon they have seen this monster," said Andrew. "They say he is colossal and coated in hair."

"Shall we go and hunt for him?" said Coral.

When they got to the woods, Andrew held back. What if they **did** see the monster?

"Come on!" said Coral. "We will be all right."

In the woods, they looked and looked, but they did not see the monster.

Then Andrew spotted something.

"Look!" he called. "A footprint."

"No," said Coral. "It is too big."

Andrew gulped. “Is it the monster’s footprint?” he said.

They ran back to the town.

“We have seen the monster’s footprints,” they yelled.

People rushed to the woods to look for the monster.

Next morning, Coral spotted a new placard.

MORNING NEWS

Some people said they had seen the monster.

"He is called Bigfoot," they said.

"We did not see him," said Coral, one of the kids.

After a few weeks, they had still not seen Bigfoot.

"I say we hunt in a new part of the woods," said Coral.

When they got to the woods, they went down a new track.

"Look!" called Andrew. "Footprints!"

"Left, right, left, right, left, **left**,"
said Coral with a frown. "That is odd."

"He must have hopped," said Andrew.

"This print has turned back on itself,"
Coral said. "It is all mixed up."

Just then, they spotted a man. He held something like a big, flat wooden sandal.

"You are printing the footprints!" said Coral.

"Correct!" said the man.

"So there is no Bigfoot?" said Coral. "It is all a hoax?"

"Oh yes," said the man with a grin. "I am the best Bigfoot hoaxer!"

Then he ran off.

Coral and Andrew turned to go back into town.

They were sad that there was no monster.

Then Coral stopped in her tracks.

"Andrew, look! Footprints!"

"They are not the hoaxer's prints," said Andrew. "They are fresh. And the hoaxer did not come this way."

A chill wind blew in the trees around them.

Thrilled, Coral and Andrew let the new trail of footprints lead the way ...

Toxic Little Critters

By Stephen Rickard

We all understand that messing with big cats or sharks is not a good plan.

However, it's not just big beasts that can do you harm.

Some of the biggest killers on the planet are little.

This little fish is "the assassin of the sea."

It lies hidden in the mud on the sea bed and waits for you to step on it.

If you do step on it, it injects its poison into you.

Without treatment, the poison can kill you.

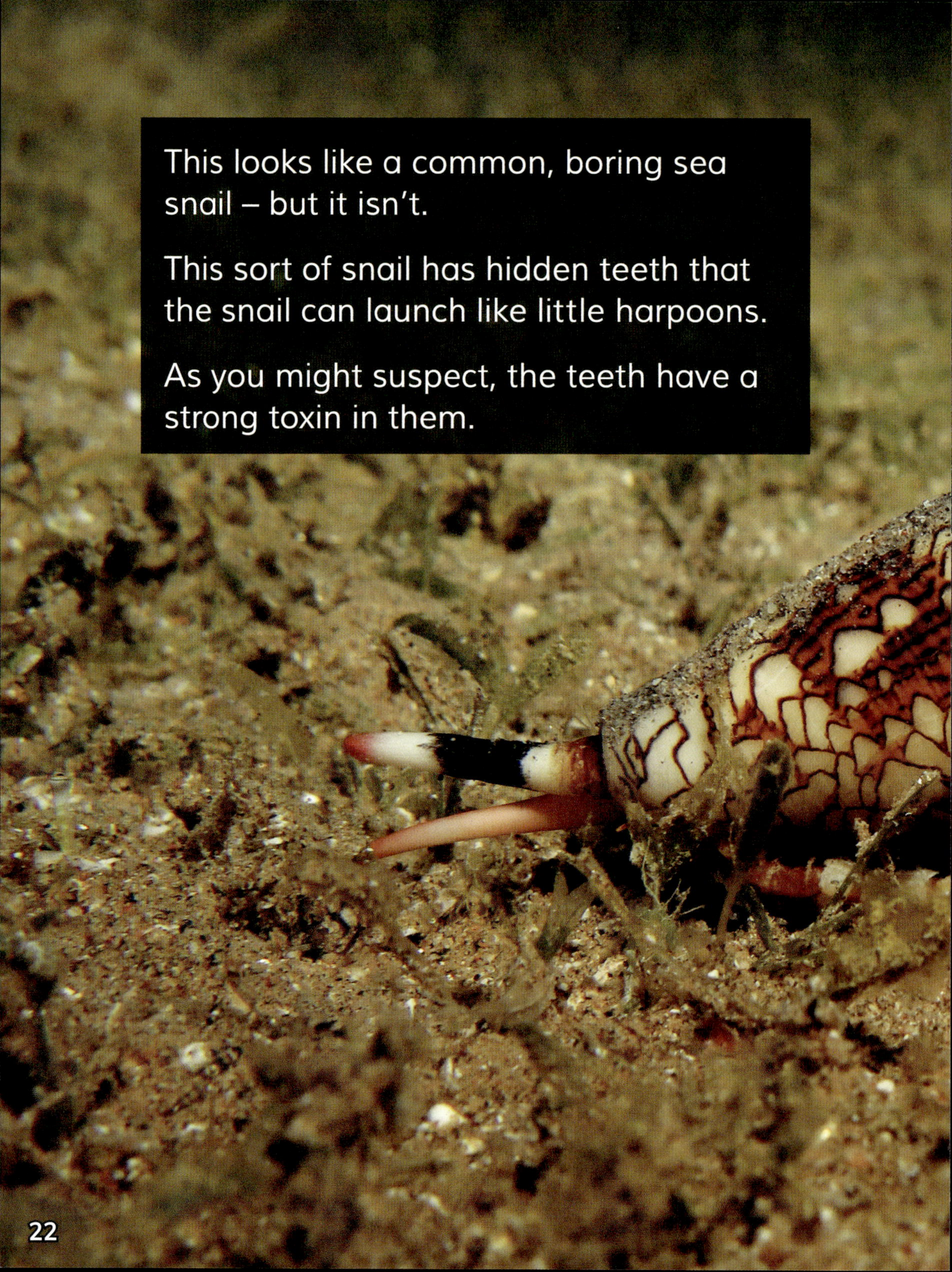

This looks like a common, boring sea snail – but it isn't.

This sort of snail has hidden teeth that the snail can launch like little harpoons.

As you might suspect, the teeth have a strong toxin in them.

The patterns on the shell are a clue.
They say, "Do not come near me!"

There are lots of poison dart frogs, but this is the one to keep clear of. It is less than an inch long, but its poison can kill at least ten adults.

Its poison glands are under its skin, so slight contact with its gooey, wet skin can kill you.

The good thing is that the poison dart frogs are all bright, so we can spot them.

It's as if they are taunting us!

This is a pufferfish and, yes, it too has toxins. So do not go near it!

People in Japan like to eat this fish. The problem is that if you eat parts containing poison, you can die.

Will you risk it?

If this mean-looking hornet stings you, you will feel a lot of pain!

The woes might not stop there, as some people can get ill and die from its sting.

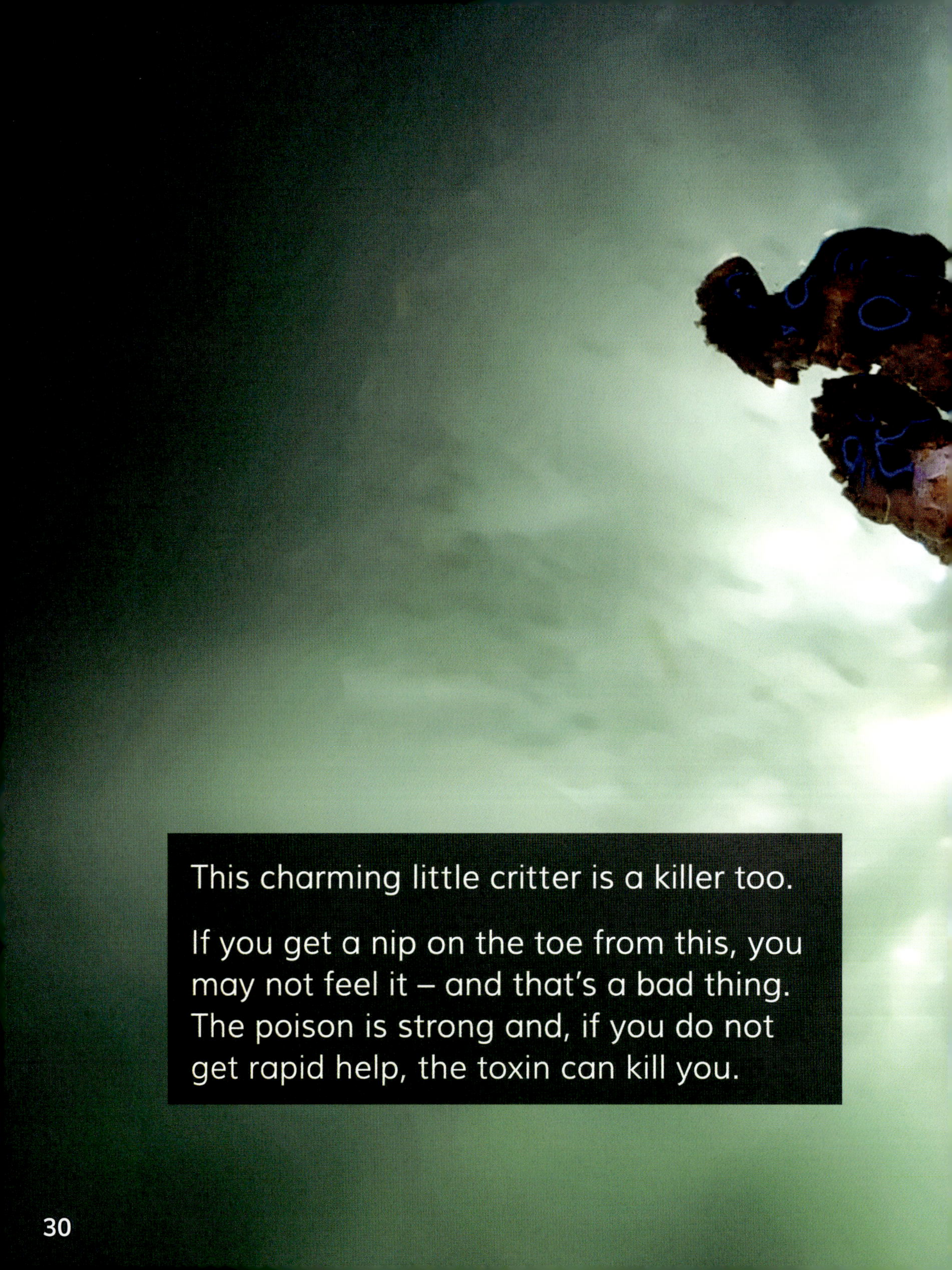

This charming little critter is a killer too.

If you get a nip on the toe from this, you may not feel it – and that's a bad thing. The poison is strong and, if you do not get rapid help, the toxin can kill you.

This little critter is the biggest little killer of all. It has no toxins, but it has lots of bad bugs in it. If we get a nip from it, we can get ill.

Each year, it infects about 700,000,000 people – and about 725,000 of them die from its nip.

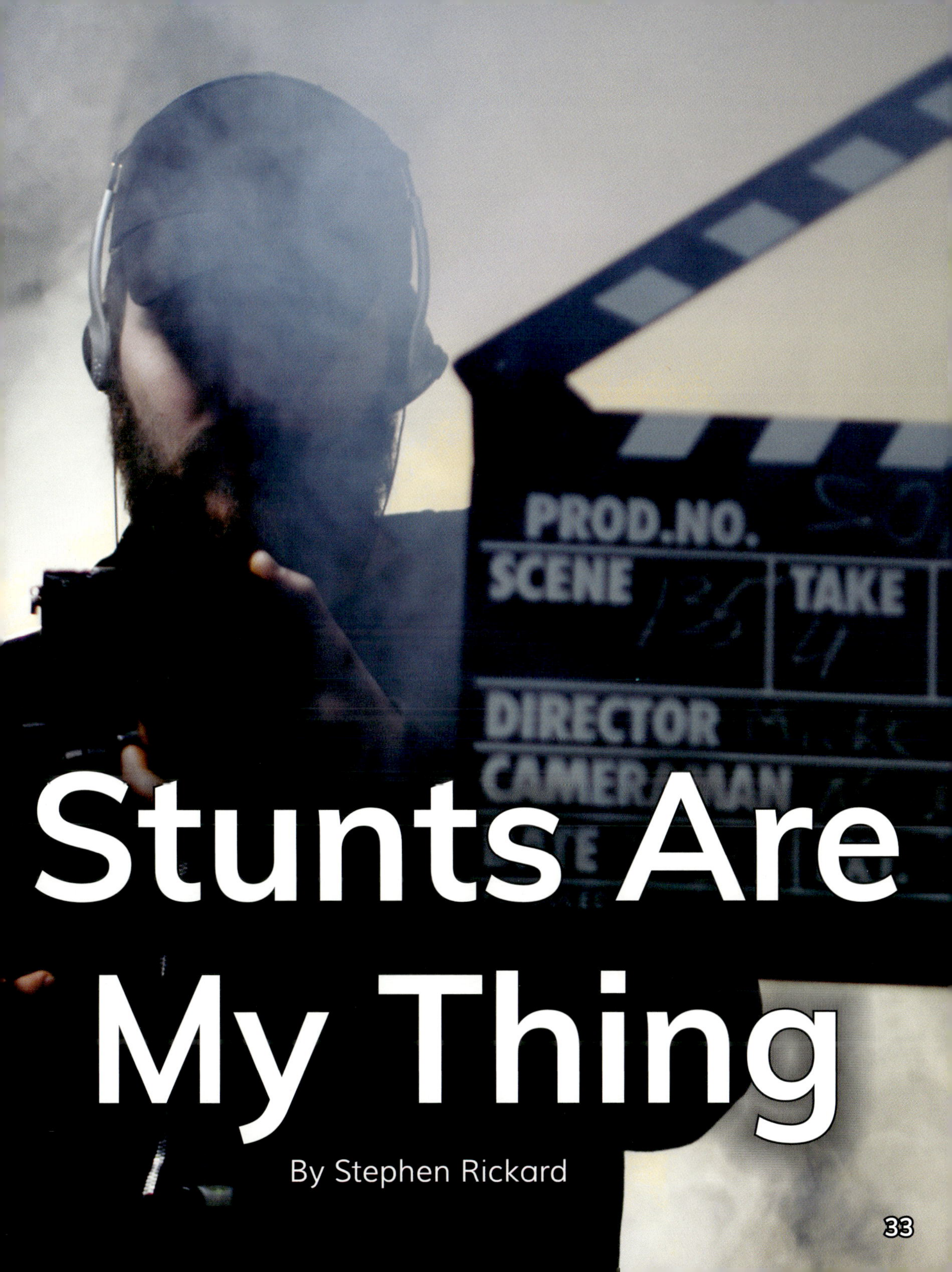

Stunts Are My Thing

By Stephen Rickard

Greetings! I'm Roscoe – and I'm a stunt man.

It's my job to stand in for actors in films, when there is high-risk stuff to do.

That's what I am paid to do.

In the film, there might be a few fights, big jumps, or traffic collisions.

When you see the film, you might think it is the actor doing this stuff, but in fact it's me.

If the main actor in a film is injured doing a stunt, you cannot just get a new actor. So all filming needs to stop.

That costs a lot!

If I get injured, it's not such a problem. They can just get a new stunt man.

Plus, I am good at keeping out of harm's way.

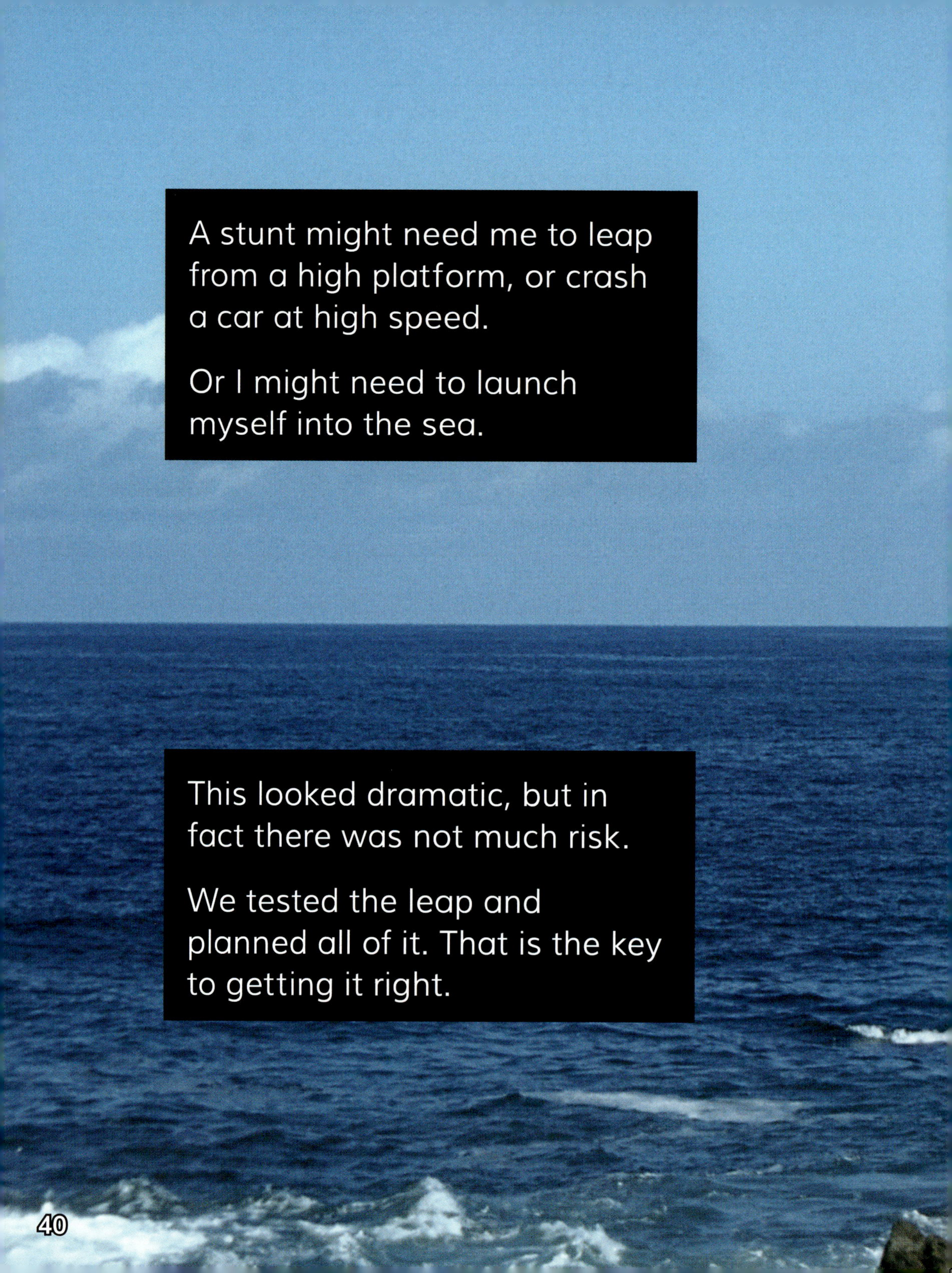

A stunt might need me to leap from a high platform, or crash a car at high speed.

Or I might need to launch myself into the sea.

This looked dramatic, but in fact there was not much risk.

We tested the leap and planned all of it. That is the key to getting it right.

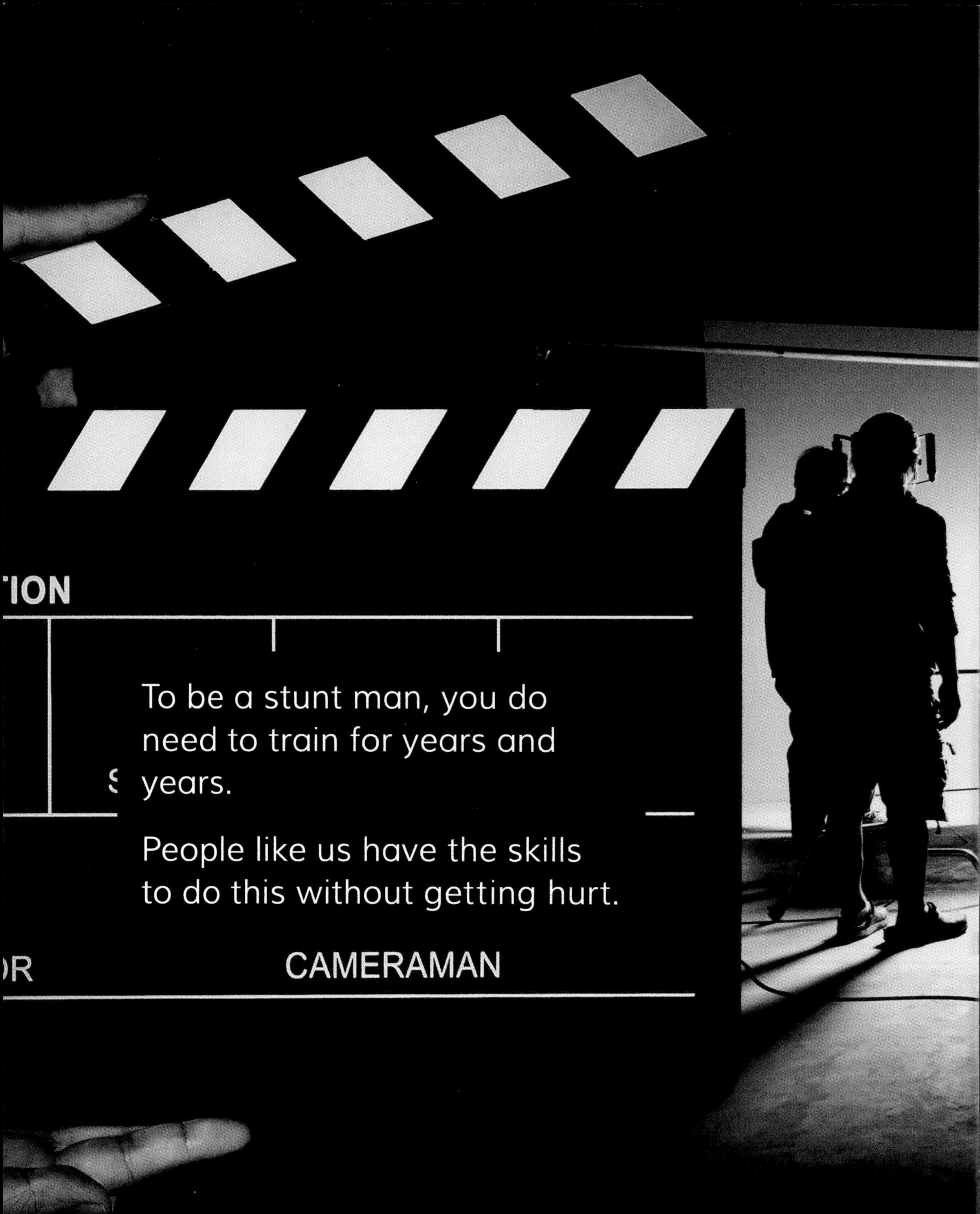

To be a stunt man, you do need to train for years and years.

People like us have the skills to do this without getting hurt.

We need vision too. We need to think of all the risks.

What things might not go well?

We have to have the right gear too.

Hauling around pads and helmets is a big part of our job.

This stunt can be a bit daunting.

For this stunt, we need lots of gear to stop our skin, throat, and lungs from getting burned.

Is this a stunt?

I do not think so. The croc might snap its jaws shut, and that is a risk I cannot avoid.

So if I was called in to do this, I'd say, "No way!"

As I said, stunts are all about planning well and avoiding risks. We never do a stunt just for fun.

So you, the reader, must never – ever – attempt a stunt.

It will not end well for you. Trust me!